OKOTOKS-

WHERE MOOSE GO SHOPPING!

AIRMAIL FROM...

OKOTOKS-
WHERE MOOSE GO SHOPPING!

Michael Cox

Illustrated by
Rhian Nest James

Scholastic Children's Books,
Commonwealth House, 1-19 New Oxford Street,
London WC1A 1NU, UK

A division of Scholastic Ltd
London ~ New York ~ Toronto ~ Sydney ~ Auckland
Mexico City ~ New Delhi ~ Hong Kong

Published in the UK by Scholastic Ltd, 1999

ISBN 0 439 01212 0

AIRMAIL FROM...

Okotoks - where moose go shopping! is part of a series of books about fascinating countries around the world. Each book is made up of letters written by a boy or girl who lives in one of these countries. You might find that their English isn't always quite right (unlike yours, which is always perfect – ha ha!). So watch out for a few mistakes and crossings out. Sometimes in their letters the children use words from their own language (just like we all do!).

You shouldn't have too much trouble with this one, though, because Keri, the writer, speaks English. But she does occasionally use a few Canadian slang words which you might find a bit strange. Don't let this bother you! Discovering the different and exciting worlds that other kids live in is exactly what these books are all about!

9 September

Dear reader

Hi! I'm Keri and I live near to a place called Okotoks which is in the province of Alberta in Canada – just about . . . here!

I was ten years old last birthday and I'm 4' 6" tall with reddy blonde hair, brown eyes and tons of freckles! Sometimes I wear glasses but most of the time I don't need to. I love animals and I'm mad on growing plants and things. My middle name is Patricia and my last one is Travis. And this is me!

I've got a 20-year-old-brother called Brad and a 6-year-old half-sister called Jodie. We live on a farm on the prairie with Glenn, Dad, and my step-mom, Carol. Carol's Jodie's mom. My real mom, Sue, lives in a town about 40 miles away from here with her new husband, Bob.

Our farm is called Bison's Leap Ranch and it's humungous. We've got three hundred cows, more than a hundred sheep, tons of hens, three dogs, two cats, five horses and about 1,000 acres of prairie land that we grow wheat on. The horses are family pets. We've got one

each and we ride them all over our ranch. Mine's called Cindy and she's a golden palomino pony with a cute blonde mane and tail. So . . . meet the Bison's Leap gang!

Labels on image: Brad, Dad, Carol, Ranch house, Cindy, Me, Jodie

This morning at school, my teacher, Miss Andrews, told us we'd gotta choose a personal

project for the year. She said it'd last until next summer and that we'd to keep a record of how we're doing. So everyone spent the next ten minutes busting their brains for ideas! Natalie Green, my best friend, decided she'd do a study of all the wild animals she sees around her dad's ranch. Frank Potter, who sits behind us, said he'd train his dog, Mack, to pull his toboggan, or learn to play the trombone. I said, "How you gonna teach a dog to play trombone, Frank?" and the whole class burst out laughing. (Frank got my joke about two hours later!)

I had no problem thinking what my project would be. I decided that I would write to you all about my life here in Canada. That way I'll be doing my project and keeping my record at the same time! Which I think is a neat idea! And, as you can see . . . I've made a start on it!

Alberta is a cool place to live! It's fall right now (I think you call it autumn). The sky's blue and the trees are covered with red and gold leaves but in a few weeks the first cold, white

flakes will fall past my bedroom window. Then we'll be getting snow, snow, snow, for at least the next six months. When November arrives nearly all Canada will be covered in snow and it'll stay like that right until next March. Don't feel sorry for me though! As well as the snow we get masses of sunshine here in Alberta. So our winters are freezing, but with lots of wicked winter sports like skiing, ice hockey, skating and tobogganing. We get great summers too. They're short, but real hot! As well, there's lots of excellent animals around here, especially in the stupendiferous Rocky Mountains, which are almost on our doorstep! Yeah, Alberta's a great place to live!

OK! I think that's enough. It's time to clean out Cindy's loose box (a sort of stable). Then I'm going to ride her over to Natalie's place. That's the next ranch to ours.

I'll write you again real soon.

Keri

20 September

Hi to you from Okotoks!

It's me, Keri. How's things in
your bit of the world? It's
harvest time here in Alberta so it's work, work,
work all the time at our place. Carol and Jodie
and me have hardly seen Dad or Brad for
weeks, they're so busy getting the wheat in. The
only time we do see them is when they run into
the kitchen for some chow — then run right
out again!

Dusk's falling right now and from my bedroom
window I can see the Rockies getting darker by

The Rockies

the second. Quite soon
they'll just be big black
shapes in the distance.
Down on the prairies,
below the Rockies, I
can see monster lights
flashing around our
fields. Yeah! Spoookeee!

It's OK though. The aliens haven't landed. The
lights are coming from the combined
harvesters and tractors! Dad, Brad and Wayne

(our ranch foreman) and all our other farm helpers are driving them. They're working their butts off to get the harvest in before it gets too cold. This is what it looks like. . .

OK! You've heard about our bit of Canada. Now it's time to tell you about the real MONSTER – I mean Canada itself. And I'm not kidding! We're the second biggest country in the world, after Russia. Just to prove how big we are, gedda load of this! My Uncle Ed and Aunt Sandra live in Vancouver on the West coast. My grown-up cousin (their daughter) Sally, lives in New Brunswick on our East Coast. When they go visit her, they drive for seven whole days! When they get there they've travelled nearly a fifth of the way around the world!

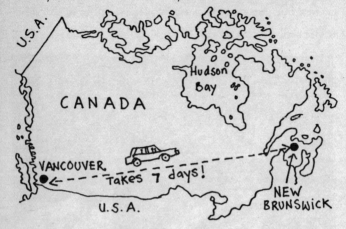

Ed and Sandra went to Britain for a holiday last year and couldn't believe how tiny it is! When they found out that it's got over 58 million people (that's twice as many as we've got) they couldn't believe it!

So - if you like wide open spaces, fantastic scenery and masses of adventure and activity stuff, you'll go crazy here. We've got humungous great forests, endless prairies, mega-mammoth mountains, more than a million lakes, plus over 52,000 islands splattered around the coast - which, by the way, is the longest in the world. And we've even got about ten zillion tons of icing on the top. That's the gigantic frozen wasteland that stretches all the way to the North Pole! Phewee! Don't you wish you lived here?

Anyway, here's a map of Canada with all this stuff marked on it:

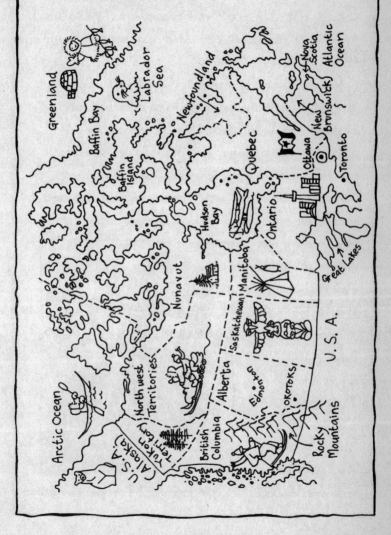

We're part of the North American Continent. Most of our people live in the south, in the big cities near the border with the USA. As you can see, our neighbour to the north-west is the USA too! That's because Alaska used to belong to Russia but America bought it off them in 1867.

How d'you like pumpkins? I grow them for fun. You see how they get bigger and bigger and bigger? They'll be ready for cutting soon. I'm going to make them into Hallowe'en lanterns for me and my pals. We have a great time here at Hallowe'en with tricks and parties and stuff. I'll tell you all about it real soon. For now, here's me with a pumpkin! I'm the one on the left!

Best wishes,

Keri

me →

pumpkin!
↓

PS Sorry about this! One more statistic to boggle your brain. I forgot to tell you that Canada's so big that we've got six time zones. So, like, when Uncle Ed and Auntie Sandra are getting out of bed at 7.30 am in Vancouver . . . in New Brunswick it's already 1.00 pm, and Sally's eating lunch!

PPS I also forgot to tell you that Canada gets its name from the Native Indian word "Kanata" – which means village or settlement.

1 October

Dear letter hound,

Hi! How ya howlin'? I think Natalie and Frank must have got kinda jealous of this pen-pal project of mine. They've asked if they can muscle in on some of my writing action. I said "Yes!" Well, what else could I do? They're my best buddies! We got together and made you a list of the top ten best things to see and do if you come to Canada.

Anyway, we all picked out our three most favourite things each for you. And instead of fighting about who got to choose number ten, we asked Miss Andrews to pick it. What did she go for? Wildlife! (She's nuts about it.)

TEN GREAT THINGS TO SEE & DO WHEN YOU COME TO CANADA

1 - Take a trip underneath Niagara Falls

<u>What are they?</u> Only the most amazing and

massive waterfalls that happen where Lake Erie overflows into lake Ontario. They're shaped like a horse shoe. Niagara is a Native Indian word that means "thunder of water". Which sounds about right!

The figures: 14 million litres of water crash over the falls every minute. That water crashes down 54 metres. That's a drop about as high as a ten-storey building! Oh, and 12 million tourists come to look at the falls every year.

Crazy fact: In 1860 a Frenchman called Blondin walked across the falls on a tightrope, stopped halfway, cooked an omelette, had a hole shot in his hat by someone in a boat below, then carried on to the other side. Waddanut! (KT)

2 - Pick up a garter snake at the Manitoba Snake Pits

<u>What goes on there?</u> Well, more red garter snakes live here than anywhere else in the world. When the snow melts in the spring, the snakes come out of their underground dens to mate. They tangle themselves into huge wriggly bunches.

<u>The figures:</u> Each bunch can have as many as 10,000 snakes all knotted up in it!

<u>Creepy fact:</u> You can pick the snakes up - if you dare! Actually, they're not dangerous. But don't take them home, they're a protected species. (KT)

YUCK GROSS!

Speak for yourself honey!!

3 - Go up the CN Tower, Toronto

<u>What is it?</u> Only the highest building in the

whole world. It transmits and receives radio and TV signals. From the top you can see things 160 kilometres away.

<u>The figures:</u> It's 553 metres high. That's over 100 metres higher than the titchy Empire State Building in New York. Ha!

<u>Crazy fact:</u> You can go up the CN Tower on the outside in a glass elevator. Then stand on the glass floor of

the observation deck and look down. Aargh! It's seriously scary! (NG)

4 - Travel back in time at the Mackenzie Bison Sanctuary

<u>What is it?</u> The nearest you'll get to finding out what life was like back in the days when meganormous herds of bison roamed the Canadian Plains.

<u>The figures:</u> There are 2,000 bison in the herd.

<u>Scary fact:</u> Don't wander about by yourself – bison can be real dangerous. (NG)

5 - Take a trip on the Canadian Pacific Railway

<u>Serious fact:</u> Before the Canadian Pacific Railway was built, Canada was like two separate countries. It was split in two by the massive Rocky mountains. European settlers tunnelled and blasted their way through the rock and stuck in a railway to link East Canada with the Pacific coast in the west.

<u>The figures:</u> The tunnels at Kicking Horse Pass are 900 metres long, but when a train goes through, its front end may be coming out while its back end is still going in! There are 150 wagons on those trains – I know, I counted 'em!

<u>Go on, take a trip:</u> It's worth it, the views are awesome-and-a-half! (FP)

6 - Find an iceberg off Newfoundland

<u>What is it?</u> Newfoundland's an island off the East coast of Canada. Humungous great icebergs the size of shopping malls float past here in the spring.

<u>Serious fact:</u> Icebergs are ginormous chunks of ice that break off the ice packs and glaciers in the cold, cold north. The Newfoundland icebergs float down from Greenland. It was an iceberg that made the Titanic sink. (Did you see the movie?)

Icebergs come in 3 varieties: "bergy bits" are the small ones; "slob ice" is kind of ice slush; and "growlers", they're the low down and dangerous ones! (KT)

<u>The figures:</u> Glaciers can churn out about 40,000 icebergs a year, but only a few hundred get as far as Newfoundland. Some icebergs are humungous! They can be about 30 metres high – that's as big as a five-storey building! (FP)

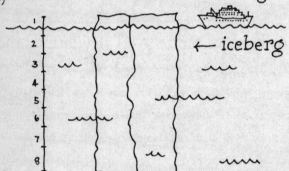

← iceberg

7 - Be dazzled by the lights at Yellowknife

<u>What are they?</u> They're pink, green, yellow and red lights that look like ribbons dancing in the sky. It's spooky and out of this world! You'll see them in northern Canada on a clear night

between December and March. They're also called the "Aurora Borealis" after the Roman goddess of the dawn! The Inuit people say the lights are the spirits of the dead people and animals. Spooky!

<u>The figures:</u> They sometimes stretch 100 kilometres into the sky!

<u>Serious fact:</u> They're caused by electrically charged particles whizzing from the sun and hitting the earth's atmosphere - at least, that's what Miss Andrews told me to say. (KT)

8 - See the midnight sunrise on Dawson's Midnight Dome

<u>What is it?</u> Midnight Dome is near Dawson City. In the winter it has months of total darkness

and in summer it's light for 24 hours a day!
<u>Crazy fact:</u> Climb to the top on Midsummer's
day (21st June) and you'll see the sun sink down
to the horizon, but it doesn't disappear, it just
comes right back up again! (NG)

9 - Go whale watching at Vancouver Island

<u>What happens here?</u> Groups of up to 20 killer
whales (orcas) come here to feed on migrating
salmon.

<u>The figures:</u> Grey whales also pass by Vancouver
island as they swim 8000 kilometres from
Mexico, where they breed, to Siberia. They
weigh between 35 and 50 tonnes and can be up
to 14 metres long - that's quite a lot bigger
than our school bus, and 3 times as heavy.

<u>Interesting fact:</u> The whales sometimes leap right out of the water and it's great to see them blowing out big spouts of water three or four times, then diving back under the waves. I came here last year and had a whale of a time! (Miss Andrews)

10 - Watch the dogsled race from Whitehorse

<u>What happens here?</u> Teams of huskies pull sleds and their drivers follow the route the old

pioneers used in the days of the Gold Rush.

The figures: The race goes all the way from Whitehorse in the Yukon to Alaska - it's 1,609 kilometres (1,000 miles) long.

Interesting fact: The Inuit first used huskies to pull their sleds when they went hunting caribou in the fall. They had to stock up on meat for the winter. (FP)

Well, waddya waitin' for? Get your folks to book you that airline ticket today!

I'll write you again soon.

Later,

Keri (and the rest of the "airmail mob")

11 October

Hi, how y'doin'?

How's your weather? It's getting real cold here.
We had a few flakes of snow the other day so
now we're all busy getting ready for the big f-
f-freeeeeze! Our apples are picked. I've
harvested my pumpkins and brought them
indoors. Well away from pesky Jack Frost! And,
most important of all, our wheat harvest is in.
Dad's real pleased! So it's happy Thanksgiving Day
to you! That's what we're havin' right now. Our
special time when we give thanks for a safe
harvest and all the good food we get from
Nature.

HAPPY THANKSGIVING !

At school this week Miss Andrews was telling us
how Thanksgiving got going in the 17th century

when the new American settlers celebrated their very first harvest.

Tonight, me and my folks will be sitting down to Thanksgiving dinner, with corn on the cob, sweet potatoes (like potatoes, but sweeter!), cranberry sauce and, of course, a huge roast turkey. We've also got two delicious desserts to look forward to – made by me! (With a little help from Carol.) What are they?

Pumpkin pie and pecan pie, naturally! Enjoy!

One of the other yummy things we'll be eating and saying thanks for is maple syrup. Have you tasted it? Hmmmm! It's so good!

(Especially spread on pancake or blobbed all over some ice-cream.) We even have a picture of a maple leaf on our national flag.

maple leaf

The Native Indians discovered maple syrup. It's made from sap taken from the trees when it flows up their trunks to the new leaves in the spring. That's why the Indians called spring the time of the Sugar Making Moon.

The guys who make the syrup cut into the tree trunk then stick a little tap in so that they can catch the sap drips in a bucket.

I would just lie under it with my mouth open.

Don't be greedy Keri, it's my turn!

mmmmm... YUMMY!

I wish we had maple trees in our backyard so I could make my own syrup but they don't grow all over Canada. Most are in Quebec and

Ontario. Some people are a bit worried that acid rain pollution is harming them. I hope not!

Try this next time it snows: find a clean patch of snow and pour hot maple syrup on to it - the syrup goes hard almost straight away. All you have to do then is pick up the maple taffy, as we call it, and eat it! Mmm!

Do you have Coffee Crimps, Fruit Rollups, Oh Henrys, Girl Scout cookies, or Captain Crunch and Lucky Charms breakfast cereals? If not, get over here quick to give 'em a try - they're wicked! I'll stop now. Got to check on that pumpkin pie!

Sweetest greetings to <u>you</u>.

Keri

PS Do you do anything like our end of harvest Thanksgiving Day?

30 October

Oooooow oooow to yooo hoooo!

It's me, Keri. That was my ghostly wailing, if you didn't guess. Spookiest greetings to you! Have you put your pumpkin Jack o' Lanterns in your windows ready to greet your Hallowe'en visitors? We have! All this week at school we've been making witches and black cats and vampires from cardboard and bits of trash. Tomorrow night, Nat and me and Frank and some other kids are going out trick-or-treating. We'll be going up to our neighbours' front doors and chanting:

We haven't always had Hallowe'en in Canada. It was brought here by the settlers who came from Europe. I know this because I've been checking out my roots. Not pumpkin ones! I've been finding out where all our people all came from as part of our school history investigation. It's fun – especially for someone as nosey as me! Here you go – check out my picture history of Canada.

Canada Kicks Off - (The Story so Far)
by K. Travis

First off our country was just gi-normous and empty and wild with stacks of (even wilder!) animals and no people. Tons of it is still <u>exactly</u> like that today!

We're all wild about Canada!

About 25,000 years ago, Stone Age hunters walked here across the frozen sea at the Bering Strait from Asia . . . here!

Over the next 20,000 years they spread all over Canada. The ones who settled in the really cold north we call the Inuit today.

The ones who settled in the south split up into smaller tribal groups. We now call them Native Indians.

We call all these first settlers and their descendants our First Nations people.

The next people to arrive were Vikings led by a guy called Lief the Lucky. He couldn't have been that lucky because after a while they went home again.

In 1497 an explorer from Britain called John Cabot arrived on our East coast. Not long afterwards the land was claimed for Britain. Just like that!

In 1534 a French explorer called Jacques Cartier turned up and he claimed the land for France! Just like that, <u>again</u>!

Both countries said the land was theirs. But over 300,000 Native Americans were already living here!

In 1689, the British and the French guys got to fighting over who should get control of Canada.

The English finally whupped the French some time around the middle of the 18th century and in the end Canada got to be part of the British Empire. But millions of French descendants still live here. In the province of Quebec four in every five people speak French. We're what's called a bilingual country. That means we've got two languages instead of one. Natalie's mom's French, by the way. Her great, great (times about 20, I guess?) grandpa was probably one of the guys fighting with the English all those years ago.

My mom says her great grandpa (times about ten squillion?) was a fur trapper in the north. The

HEY! Where'd you get that hat?

white settlers first came here to trap animals for their fur so they could sell it for big prices back in Europe. Beaver skin hats were real cool in those days. Not any more, the beavers will be glad to tell you!

Dad's family have been here hardly any time at all next to Mom's. They came to Canada from Britain about a 100 years ago. My English great, great grandpop saw a poster that said something like, "Britishers! Bring your families to Canada. Only $15 Ocean Fare. Children under 17 years free!" And the Canadian government were giving 160 acres of land in Alberta to anyone who wanted to have a go at farming it. For free! Guess what great, great grandpop called his ranch? Yup, Bison's Leap! Way to go!

Ton ami (your friend),

Keri

PS Maybe some of your ancestors emigrated to Canada. You never know . . . I might even know some of their descendants!

1 November

Happy Hallowe'en

Bonjour to you!

So how was Hallowe'en? We've had stacks of fun here at Okotoks. We always do! Hallowe'en is the second biggest holiday festival of the year in Canada. (Christmas is the biggest.)

Hallowe'en's not just for us kids either. The grown-ups join in the fun! The best bit around here is the excellent competition where everyone tries to make their house look scary and haunted. When we've all done spookifying up our homes, a gang of judges goes from one house to the other, deciding which one freaks them most. At our house we hung up the creepy spiders and stuff we'd made at school, then sprayed a mess of pretend cobwebs around the rooms.

Me and Jodie thought it looked wicked. Don't think Carol was too impressed though. She said she'd be the one who'd have to clean it all up afterwards. Give me a break! Guess which house won this year? Frank Potter's! The judges said the head on the kitchen table was seriously scary.

They were also real terrified by the blood curdling moaning and howling they could hear all the time they were walking around the Potter place. It was Mack! Frank's dad had shut him in their basement just before the judges arrived.

Ooooow!

I'll sign off now. I've got a great chunk of history homework to get my teeth into!

Keri

PS Have you got a cellar? Loads of people have got them here. Our ground gets frozen real hard quite deep down in winter. Our big tough basements stop our houses sinking down when the soil goes soft again in the spring.

Only Kidding! They don't really go this deep!

They're also useful in lots of other ways. Our basement has got our central heating furnace in it and a huge games room with a pool table and a juke box! Neat, huh?

Juke box

Boiler

Pool table

PPS Some really cool news! Cindy's going to have a foal next spring. I can't wait!

4 November

Dearest pen-pardner,

Hey! How are you? And how's school? Do you get a fall term break? I wish we did. I'm feeling real jealous this week because, while I'm stuck in class, that lucky big brother of mine, Brad, has gone off on holiday with Jane, his girlfriend. Not fair! They're up at Churchill in Manitoba Province on a polar-bear-watching trip. Lucky them! It sounds like a wicked trip. We got a letter today and I thought you'd like to hear about it too – so here it is:

Dear Dad, Carol, Keri and Jodie,
Arrived safely. Churchill is a pretty stripped-down sort of town — no trees, no pavements, no traffic lights — but the arctic scenery is <u>awesome!</u> Tomorrow we're off out in a tundra buggy to do some bear watching.

But listen to this! This afternoon we were strolling around town when Jane suddenly grabbed my arm and screamed, "Brad, there's a polar bear coming towards us!" She wasn't joking! Walking down Main Street, there was this massive polar bear! Well, two, actually. By this time its big buddy had joined it.

They were huge! They had paws as big as my head! I think our noses probably came halfway up their chests. But we didn't wait to find out. We ran into a store. The guy behind the counter had already seen the bears and was on the phone to the authorities when we rushed in. Later we found out that bears often wander round the town at this time of year. So there's an emergency code to call if you see them. It's B.E.A.R! Not too hard to forget – even if you are in a panic!

After about five minutes some official-looking guys turned up and asked about the bears. We told them, "They went thattaway!" and they took off after them.

"What will they do when they catch them?" I asked the store owner.

"Arrest them. Then put them in jail, of course!" he said.

"You're kidding!" I said.

"Nope!" he laughed. "We got our own polar bear jail just outside town. They'll keep them there for a while then take them out on to the ice and release them."

"But only for good bearhaviour?" said Jane. (Ha ha!)

So! The bears found us before we found them!

Love to you all,

Brad and Jane

PS I'm bringing back a couple of polar bear cubs for Keri and Jodie!

Wow scareeey! I wouldn't like to come face to face with a couple of enormous polar bears

 on Main Street, would you? I've just looked up polar bears in my animal encyclopaedia. Did you know that most of all the world's polar bears live in our Arctic regions? We've got about 25,000 altogether. I didn't know that! In the winter, the Manitoba ones go on to the frozen sea in Hudson Bay and hunt seals. They're specially made for it. They can jump and climb real well and can swim underwater with just the tip of their nose showing. When they see a likely-looking victim they suddenly <u>blast</u> out of the water like a rocket – so watch out you seals!

They can really run, too. They've got hair all over the pads of their paws to stop them slipping over. And they've got a great sense of smell.

They can even sniff out seals who are hiding under ice, even when it's a metre thick. And spookiest of all, they can pick up our human smell from 32 kilometres away!

Hmm... I smell a little girl!

My own awesome sense of smell has just told me that dinner is being dished up just 15 metres away. So I'll make my way down to the kitchen!

Best wishes,

Keri

PS D'you think Brad was kidding about the baby polar bears?

3 December

Howdy pal,

It's me, Keri. How's you? Looking forward to your Christmas vacation? Me too! What presents are you hoping for? I've got fingers crossed for some clothes for me and a new saddle for Cindy.

D'you think you'll get a white Christmas? If not, you can have some of our snow. It's been falling non-stop for three days so we've got tons and tons of it! Yesterday Brad and me spent ages clearing our backyard with the snow blower. When we got up this morning all our hard work had disappeared under another fall of the cold white stuff.

The temperature outside is -20°C at the moment. Every time I go out the door I have to wrap up in about ten billion layers of clothes and put on my snow suit, mittens and toque (woollen hat). Did you know that you lose most of your body heat from the top of your head? (I didn't! Dad told me a couple of minutes ago.)

Guess who?

I wear my sunglasses sometimes, to stop the glare from the snow dazzling me. Then it's scrunch, scrunch, scrunch across the freezing yard to pick up some firewood from our log stack or to check that Cindy's OK.

This morning I was carrying a bucket of water to Cindy's stable and some of it spilled. It froze solid almost <u>before</u> it hit the ground. <u>That</u>'s how cold it is here! In the north it's even colder. The "north" is what us Canadians call all of the North West and the Yukon Territories that stretch all the way up to the North Pole. It's massive, it's frozen, and hardly anyone lives there. Sometimes the temperature up there drops so low that it can make metal shatter into little pieces! Do you believe it?

In the north they have frost all year round. But it's not frost you can see all the time. It's called permafrost and in the summer it's hidden under the ground. As well as being icy cold, the climate in the north is also very dry. So, believe it or not, they don't get nearly as much snow as we do. But of course, the snow that does fall, doesn't melt.

Our southern snow is coming down even heavier now. I think I'll put another log on the fire and snuggle up in front of the TV for a couple of thousand years.

Warmest wishes from your <u>very best</u> pen-pal,

Keri

PS Brad did bring me and Jodie a couple of polar bear cubs. But they were cuddly toy ones! I should've guessed. Anyway, they're real cute!

8 December

Yo de ho from the land of snow,

It's me, Keri. How's it going? Listen to this! All us kids were having a mega-massive snowball battle yesterday when we had a bit of an emergency. Jodie had, like, got bored with the snowballing and wandered off but the rest of us were so into the fight that we didn't notice. After we'd just about snowballed ourselves stupid, Natalie said, "Hey! Where's Jodie?" So we all went quiet and tried to remember when we'd last seen her. That's when we heard crying coming from behind our big barn. We rushed around the corner and found her. She was stuck to the metal rail we tie the horses to. And this is what she looked like!

Booo hoo!

No way! She was stuck to the rail by her <u>tongue</u>! When she'd got fed up with the snowballing she'd decided to lick the metal. And her tongue got frozen to it! She was stuck there for at least five minutes. In the end Carol came to the rescue! She poured warm water on to Jodie's tongue to unfreeze it. That's the only way to do it. Dad said if it happened again we wouldn't bother rescuing Jodie, she'd just have to stay like that until the spring thaw came. Dad likes his little jokes.

Anyway, Carol brought out some fresh fruit juice. And soon we were all making slurpies and Jodie forgot about the whole thing!

Snowballing and slurpies and metal-rail-licking (if you're Jodie!) aren't the only fun us kids have at this time of year. I love to go sledding. . .

Whizzing down hills on bits of old plastic or cardboard. Best when the hills are covered with holes and lumps. But also painful and dangerous! When the snow banks get higher we tunnel into them to make forts. It's Snow Wars! When a rival gang attacks we pelt them with a zillion snowballs.

Wheeeee!

If we didn't get snow in winter we'd all be bored stupid. I mean, we couldn't spend the <u>whole</u> winter watching TV could we? (Well, maybe!) Gonna have to stop now - I've got my school work to do!

Best wishes and a thousand flying snowballs to you,

Keri

PS Hey! I've just thought. Maybe you don't know how to make slurpies? They're easy! Here's what you do. Take the top off your juice box. Turn it upside down and empty the juice into the fresh snow. There's your slurpie! Now all you do is eat it! You need <u>real</u> clean and <u>real</u> fresh snow for slurpies. Not that yukky stuff you get on city pavements (uurgh, gross!).

14 December

Dear ice fiend,

Howdy doody doo . . . to you! You started your
gift buying yet? Here in Alberta we're mega-
busy getting ready for Christmas. We've just
got back from a three day Christmas shopping
trip in Edmonton, the biggest city in the
province.

   Edmonton's perfect for this mega-shop because
it's got West Edmonton Mall. Have you heard of
it? It's awesome! The biggest indoor shopping
centre in the <u>whole world</u>! It's gigantiferous -
covering an area the size of 115 American
football fields! With 800 shops, an amusement
park <u>and</u> Fantasyland Hotel. That's where we

stayed. For our Christmas treat, me and Jodie got to choose which theme we wanted for our room. This year we stayed in the Igloo suite. We slept in a snow house on the tundra and had baths inside an iceberg. (All pretend, of course!)

The Igloo Suite

Our Bedroom!

The Bathroom!

It was all real cool. (Well, sort of!) Last year we stayed in the Truck suite. Our bed was the front seat of a monster truck and there were working traffic lights and old-fashioned gas (I think you call it petrol) pumps in our room.

West Edmonton Mall is a real hyper-massive indoor city! And I guess _that_ makes a whole lotta sense when winter's as cold as ours! Dad reckons you could stay in there for years and _never_ ever have to go out.

I don't think he would though. He's too much of an outdoors guy. But that doesn't stop him staying hours on the indoor golf course! Carol thinks the Mall's great because she can, like, hire a motor scooter and shop herself brainless that way!

The best part for me is the indoor amusement park. That's the biggest in the world too! The rides are just horrendible! Could you handle these two? In The Drop of Doom you're strapped in a cage. Then you fall 13 floors in just a few seconds! Are you kidding?

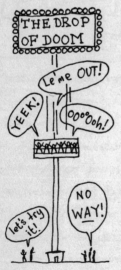

And the Mindbender triple loop roller-coaster is 14 floors high! It's the world's biggest! (Of course!)

Brad loves it! But he's a real dare-devil (and

a show off!).

Jodie and me think the World Waterpark's real cool! It's got 22 waterslides, three whirlpools, a long beach with crashing waves, palm trees, real sand and the world's only indoor bungee jump! Wicked!

Uh oh! I've just thought of another great thing in the Mall. The not-to-be-missed Deep Sea Adventure. If you go for all that underwater stuff, you can take a ride in one of its fleet of four submarines (that's more than the whole Canadian Navy's got!) and see the 200 different kinds of fish, seals and penguins that swim around in the world's biggest indoor lake!

Hi!

Tempted? Bet you are! OK . . . I'll shut up about it now. To be honest with you though, after all the rushing around and the crowds in Edmonton, I really was glad to get back to good old Okotoks and the peace and quiet of the countryside and wide open spaces of our ranch.

The <u>biggest</u> best wishes in the world,

Keri (and the rest of the Mall rats!)

PS A buck is our nickname for a dollar. Years ago the Native Indians swapped buckskins (deer skins) with the Europeans who gave them whiskey and guns. Yup, they used the skins as money. That's why the dollar's called a buck all over North America. Confession – I just looked this up in a book!

16 December

Hey there pal!

How ya doin'? Is it all systems go at your school
right now? It is at ours! We're doing Christmas
plays, carol singing, parties . . . all kinds! We're
real busy so I'll keep this letter short!

In between all this hard work me and Nat did
manage to go snow-shoeing across the fields
around our ranches so that she could check
out some wild stuff for her project. Do you use
snow shoes? The Native Indians invented them
and they're excellent! You can walk on really
deep snow in them and you won't fall through it.

Have a great Christmas vacation,

Best wishes,

Keri

A Merry Christmas to You !

To my new penfriend and family
Have a great festive season and
all good wishes for your
New Year!
from
Keri-Travis &
family

22 December

Dear you,

Do you like your photocard? Yes, that is me on the sleigh with Dad, Carol, Jodie and Brad. And the horse pulling it is Cindy. Sleigh riding is my number one thing to do at Christmas. We wrap up warm then go visiting friends and family and delivering presents. Cindy trots along with her hooves making a groovy, soft, padding noise in the snow and the sleigh bells jingle while we wave to our neighbours and shout "Merry Christmas!" as we pass them.

Santa Claus must feel just like us when he's on his rounds. I wish I could visit you on our sleigh and bring you a gift. But you're a bit too far away. I guess I'll have to leave that to Santa!

Nat and I saw this weird sight in the snow!

Have an absolutely <u>awesome</u> Christmas without me.

I'll write you early in the New Year,

Love,

Keri

PS Those animals you can see in the background of our photocard are elk. (So now you know!)

8 January

Dearest pen-pal,

Hi! It's me – Keri! Happy New Year to you. Did
you get what you wanted for Christmas? I did!
My best things were the saddle for Cindy (yes, I
got it!) and some real neat clothes from Mum.

Jodie got stacks of clothes too, but
she says her best thing is her Inuit
doll.

I spent New Year's at Mom's place.
It was great. Except when I had to leave. Then
we were both really sad (lots of sobs all round!).

We're having a Chinook today. Sounds like a
celebration, doesn't it? It's not . . . it's a wind!
This morning there were 18 centimetres of snow
on our yard and the temperature was 15° below

freezing. Then by lunch it
was as warm as spring and
the snow had nearly all
melted. And that was all
because of the Chinook!
It's a really warm wind
and it comes whipping over
the Rockies from the

Pacific Ocean. Before you can say "skimpy swimsuits!" it can make the temperature here go up by as much as 40°C. It's like going from winter to summer in just a couple of hours. No wonder the Indians called it the Snow Eater!

Alberta's the only place in the whole world where you get Chinooks. So _you_ can't have one. Get your own wind. (Only joking!) Other parts of Canada have their own special winds too. On Ellesmere Island in the north they have one called the Cow Storm. It's supposed to be so strong that it blows the horns off the musk oxen! You gotta be kidding!

I'll write you again soon.

Best wishes,

Keri

26 January

Is there anyone out there . . . are you
receiving me. . .? Are you receiving me. . .?
  Hi! It's Keri. With your letter f-f-f-from f-f-
f-freezing Alberta in c-c-c-cold C-C-C-C-
Canada. Brrrr. Yes, it's pretty frosty here! This
morning our outdoor thermometer was on -26°C.
Right now I'm nice and warm sitting at my desk
writing your letter but looking from my window I
can see Dad and Brad and Mr Potter (Frank's
dad) trying to like dig our pick-up out
of a meganormous snowdrift.

  While it's been so cold I've been doing the
First Nations bit of my Canada topic. I've just
finished the Inuit part. They really are a bunch
of tough cookies! They must be, otherwise they
couldn't have stayed alive for thousands of

years in what is about the unfriendliest place on earth. I mean, it's cold down here in southern Canada, but at least the settlers here had forests full of timber for fuel and building, and good soil for growing food. Up there in the north the Inuit had nothing but snow, ice and wild animals!

I've found out loads about the Inuit so I thought it would be fun to make you an Inuit mini-quiz. Brad helped me cook up the questions. So have a go, or he'll go into a super-sulk! And by the way, be warned! Sometimes my big brother's a real joker! I'll stick the quiz answers at the end of the letter. (No peepin'!)

Old Days Inuit Mini Quiz by K.&B. Travis.

All you have to do is pick out which one is the wrong answer to each of these questions!

1. At one time all the Inuit were nomadic. This means:

a) They lived underground. True/false?

b) They wandered around following the wild critters that they needed for food. True/false?

c) They often moved house and spent the winter in ice houses called igloos and the summer in tents made from animal skins. True/False?

2. The Inuit travelled. . .
a) On sleds pulled by dogs. True/False?
b) In canoes made from animal skins. True/False?
c) By sitting on small icebergs and paddling with their hands. True/False?

3. The first thing an Inuit hunter did when he returned with food was. . .
a) Share it with all the families in his village group. His own family ate last and got the smallest share. True/False?
b) Throw it up in the air so everyone had to make a mad dash for it. Whoever got it, ate

it! True/false?

4. The Inuit were brilliant at making do. If they couldn't find anything else. . .

a) They made the cross-bars for their sleds from caribou bones. True/false?

b) They played ice hockey using really big icicles and frozen polar bear poo. True/false?

c) They made sled runners from frozen fish wrapped in sealskin. True/false?

5. When Inuit were hunting these were the tricks they pulled on the animals:

a) They built big piles of rocks that looked like giant men so that the animals ran towards the real hunters who'd be waiting to bump them off! True/false?

b) As they approached the animals they walked

backwards to make them think they were really going in the opposite direction. True/false?

6. Animals provided almost all the food the Inuit got so. . .

a) They ate all of the parts they could possibly get down including eyeballs, heart, guts, the whole thing! True/false?

b) They usually ate the animals raw because there was hardly any fuel for cooking. True/false?

c) In a special ceremony to celebrate the arrival of spring the Inuit cooked and ate their old clothes. True/false?

7. OK! Last of all some teasers about Inuit clothes and stuff:

a) To make animal skins soft enough for boots

and stuff Inuit women chewed them and often wore their teeth down to stumps. True/false?

b) To decorate their faces in the old days Inuit women threaded animal gut covered in soot through their skin. Yuk! True/false?

c) When Inuits came to some sort of agreement they swapped clothes made from seal skins. To "seal" the deal. That's how we get the word! True/false?

I like your new boots.

Thanks!

Easy . . . or what! Now, it's time for you to talk Inuit! If you go hunting with your pal and have a quarrel over a missed shot, you say this:

Tuktvsiuriagatigit ΦiƞgnapinngitkyΦtinnga!

How's that for a mouthful? It means:

You'll never go caribou hunting with me again!

When you make friends with your hunting pal, why not share some real Inuit ice-cream with them. Here's the recipe for it:

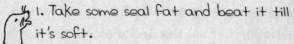

1. Take some seal fat and beat it till it's soft.

2. Melt it in a pan until you've got some good thick grease.

3. Take some roe (eggs) from an Arctic char (a sort of salmon) and some berries from the nearest bush (if you can find one!).

4. Grind them up together and stir them slowly into the grease and add some salt.

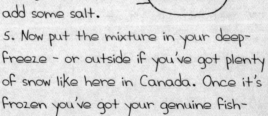

5. Now put the mixture in your deep-freeze – or outside if you've got plenty of snow like here in Canada. Once it's frozen you've got your genuine fish-flavoured Inuit ice-cream! Yum!

I guess a lot of modern day Inuit people eat the ordinary sort of ice-cream we buy in the supermarket. Since the Europeans arrived the

Inuit lifestyle has changed a lot. Nowadays they live in wooden houses and travel about on snowmobiles but still hunt and fish as they did in the old days.

Remember what I said about the Europeans taking the land from the Indians and the Inuit? On 1 April 1999 our government gave 200,000 (two hundred thousand) square kilometres back to the Inuits. About time too! It used to be part of the North West Territories. It covers one-fifth of all Canada.

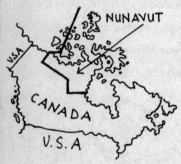

It's new name is Nunavut.

By the way, some people call the Inuit Eskimos. Eskimo really means "eater of raw flesh". Inuit means "The Only People".

Best wishes,

Keri

OK! Here are the quiz answers:

1. a) is false   2. c) is false
3. b) is false   4. b) is false
5. b) is false   6. c) is false
7. c) is false

12 February

Dear envelope ripper,

Hi! How ya doin'? Do you play games and sport much? In Canada everyone's games and activities mad! But what would you do if you lived in a region that has endless nights, blizzards that last for days and you're stuck in a small space (like an igloo) with no proper sports gear? Then you'd be like the Inuit, and these are the sort of games you'd end up inventing.

The Inuit Olympics

Aaaargh! pant! puff! Neeeargh!

<u>The Head Pull</u> – Two big strong Inuit guys (or women) lie face to face. Their heads are joined by a canvas strap. They both tug in opposite directions but can't touch the strap with their hands. The first one to pull the other one's head across the line is the winner!

There's a different version of this game called the Mouth Pull and one called the Ear Pull - you can imagine what happens here!

<u>The Ear Lift</u> - A really heavy weight is looped on to someone's ear. They have to walk as far as they can carrying the weight with just their ear.

<u>The One Foot High-Kick</u> - They hang something like a sealskin from a pole a couple of metres above the ground. Then someone has to jump into the air and kick it. Yup, it's a tricky one!

<u>Knuckle Hops</u> - You have just your knuckles and toes touching the floor with your body stretched out between them. Then you have to sort of hop your body across the floor. It makes a terrible mess of your knuckles.

OUCH!

<u>Blanket Tossing</u> - This one's my favourite. Someone gets on a blanket made from seal or walrus skin, then all the other Inuit people grab the edges and lift them up. The person on the blanket bounces into the air as high as they can. Everyone takes turns and the winner is the one who bounces highest. Neat, huh?

Any of these take your fancy? I hope not!

The really big outdoor activities that I've not mentioned yet are our rodeos. Now, they really are <u>something else</u>! You'll have to hang on for details in a few months' time. Yahoo!

Best wishes,

Keri

22 March

Hi! How y' doin?

    I've just <u>got</u> to tell you about what happened yesterday. I guess you'll probably think it's real funny! But <u>I</u> didn't think so at the time.

    Frank Potter's got this crazy idea to train Mack for search and rescue. The snow's started melting so we all went off to the woods to try him out. When we got into the really thick bit of the forest, Frank said, "Stay!" to Mack. Then we all ran off and hid. After a

woof!

few minutes Frank whistled and yelled "Find us Mack! Find us boy!" But Mack didn't quite get the idea. Instead of coming to look for us, <u>he</u> ran off and hid too! Some dumb dog!

    Well, after a while we came out and started hunting for him. Mack may have been useless at searching but he was <u>excellent</u> at hiding. After ten minutes we still couldn't find him. Then, all of a sudden, I saw some black fur sticking out from behind a tree and shouted, "Gotcha Mack, you

crazy mutt!" and I pounced on him. Except it
wasn't Mack. It was a
skunk! The skunk wasn't
too pleased. It let me
have it with both barrels!
I was drenched from head
to toe in skunk stink! If
you've never smelled a
skunk, imagine all the most yukky stinks you've
ever smelled, mix them up, make them at least
fifty times stronger and you'll be somewhere
near to what I smelled like yesterday!

On the way home, Frank, Natalie and Mack
(who'd come to see what the fuss was about)
wouldn't come near me. It was so unfair!

Tomato Juice

When I got back, Carol
had a real good moan at
me then made me take a
bath in tomato juice. I
couldn't believe it, after
all I'd been through, but
Carol said that's about the only thing that gets
rid of the stink! Gimme a break!

Skunks apart, we've got masses and masses of
great wildlife. So here, to give you some idea of
all the stuff that's creeping, galloping and

leaping around, Nat and I are proud to present. . .

Keri & Nat's Great Canadian Creature Feature – Part One

SKUNK Looks like a big black cat but it's got a big white stripe down its back and a huge bushy tail.

<u>Where found</u> – The woods, parks in cities, backyards, all over the place. Even in your trash can! So watch out!

<u>Interesting facts</u> – They eat plants, insects and other little creatures. <u>Not</u> my favourite furry friend.

ELK They're the big deer we sometimes call wapiti. Do you remember these guys from your Christmas card?

<u>Where found</u> – Around the Rockies and in the woods. Sometimes they come into the fields and make my dad unhappy by eating his crops.

<u>Interesting facts</u> – The stags grow mega-huge antlers which fall off each spring. We've got a set on our barn wall.

They're really useful for hanging coats and horse bridles and things on. When they're attached to an elk they're also used for butting Canadians with. We have to be real careful of males in the mating season. Moms with calves can be dangerous too.

MOOSE

Easy to recognize. They are

absolutely enormoose (ha!). Nearly two metres just to their shoulders. That's as tall as my dad!

<u>Where found</u> – Their best places to hang out are swamps and

79

forests. In October and November we hear them bellowing in the woods. You'll see road signs warning drivers of "moose on the loose" - they don't know their highway code! Sometimes they call into town. A couple of winters' ago, Nat and me spotted a great big bull moose out back of our local mini-mart. He had up-ended a trash-can and was munching through a load of rotten vegetables

Hmm, not a bad deal!

and stuff. I guess he was just shopping!

<u>Interesting facts</u> - Their antlers are humungous and they have that dangly skin-flap called a bell just below their chin. The Native Indians used to eat them and make clothes from their skins.

COYOTES - These are a type of wild dog.

<u>Where found</u> - On the prairies. The sun's just setting here so I can hear a pack of them singing their hearts out

as I'm writing you this.

<u>Interesting facts</u> – They make a sort of yipping
and howling noise. A "Yippee Aye . . . Coyote Ay!"
sort of thing. It'll never make the charts! Like
all the ranchers around here, Dad absolutely
hates them because they like kill and eat our
young sheep and cattle whenever they get a
chance.

BEAVER – Bet you know these! They're our

national animal.
<u>Where found</u> – You'll
see them on our ponds
and lakes. And on the
back of our nickels
(our five-cent coin)!

<u>Interesting facts</u> – They're real smart little
guys. When they want to knock up a new home
in the woods they get as busy as err . . .
beavers?! They gnaw away at a tree trunk until
the tree falls across a river and catches all
the stuff drifting downstream. The beavers add
sticks and stones and mud to it for strength
until they've got a real neat dam. Next they
build a lodge house upstream from the dam, or
on the river-bank with a roof made of sticks.

Then they start cutting young trees (their favourite chow) and storing them at the bottom of the pond. Hey presto! They've got a well-stocked larder and nice cosy waterside home to spend the winter in!

OK! That's it for now - I've saved some of the rarer and more ornery (our slang for naughty) animals for part two. So watch this Rocky mountainside!

Keri

PS The weather here is warming up. I've spotted some green and brown patches where the snow has melted. Doesn't mean it won't snow again, though. We sometimes get snow falls in April and May. And even as late (or early?) as August! Dad doesn't mind. They help water his crops.

5 April

Hiyah buddy!

Did you like my Creature Feature letter? Today in class Miss Andrews got to telling us that there used to be tons more wildlife in Canada than now. Even though the Native Indians and Inuits hunted wild animals for food and clothing and shelter they only killed what they needed to stay alive.

 When the white settlers got here from Europe the wildlife began to vanish real fast. Almost as soon as they arrived they got busy with guns and traps, turning thousands and thousands of animals like beavers and foxes into fur coats and hats for themselves and their buddies back in Europe. And sometimes, believe it or not, they went out and just wasted hundreds of animals . . . for kicks!

Miss Andrews told us about one famous guy who got real bothered about so many of our wild animals disappearing. His Indian name was Wha-Sha-Quon-Asin – but most people called him Grey Owl. Here's a picture of him.

Grey Owl spent his time writing best-selling books and magazine articles about how the Native Indians felt about nature. Their idea was that we should take only what we need and always respect it. He travelled in America and England, giving talks to important people about it. He even went to see the King of England and his daughter Princess Elizabeth to give them the word. People everywhere said this Native Indian was a very great and special man. Then, in 1938, he died – and everyone got a real big shock!

Grey Owl wasn't really Grey Owl at all. He wasn't even a Native Indian! He was really an Englishman called Archibald Stansfield Belaney. When Archibald was a young boy he'd got really fed up with the very bossy Aunt he lived with. So he'd run away from home and ended up here in Canada. After that, he had masses of adventures in the great outdooors and kind of turned himself into a new Native Indian person. He fooled everyone else too!

Talking of the great outdoors, in a few weeks' time me and Natalie are off for a short road trip with Mom and Bob. We're going to the Rocky Mountains.

Wahoo!

Wildest wishes,

Keri

PS I wasn't kidding about the animals being killed for kicks. The white hunters used to shoot hundreds and hundreds of bison from the windows of train carriages then just leave their bodies to rot on the prairies. Gross, eh? I think they were all just a bunch of sickos!

15 April

Hi mooseface,

How's things? Mom phoned the other day and said she'd seen a blackbird collecting twigs to build its nest, so maybe spring is here at last! Any signs of spring where you live? If there are, maybe you're feeling like whooping it up a bit to celebrate?

Most Canadians go a little crazy when spring arrives. Especially the ones who live in the north. Can you blame 'em? Sometimes, in icy weather, some northerners get trapped indoors for weeks and weeks on end and they can get something called cabin fever.

If I don't get out soon I'm gonna go crazy!

To make up for it Canadians organize all sorts of crazy capers any chance they get. Frank and Natalie and I have all been to some real freaky festivals so between us we've made you a calendar of our faves. Be warned! Some of the events are completely wacky! Look on the picture map to see where they all happen.

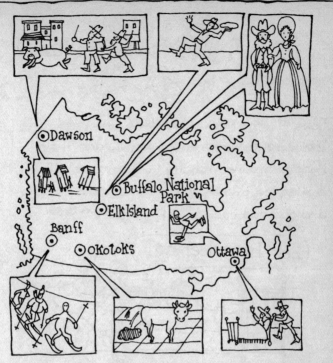

Now for the calendar. Hope you like it. Count the nuts on the wackometer for marks out of ten for wackivity.

Keri

Ps I hope you don't mind me calling you mooseface. I don't really mean it (or do I?). Just getting a little crazy I guess!

Coyote-features

A Calendar of Crazy

FEBRUARY

The Ottawa Winterlude - people race their buddies around the city in their beds! Plus mind-blowing ice and snow sculptures, speed skating and dog-sled racing. **F.P.** ◒◒◒◒◒◒

MARCH

Dawson St Patrick's Day Celebrations - My favourite event is the pig racing competition - two-man teams race their prize porkers down the main street of town. **F.P.** ◒◒◒◒◒◒◒◒◒

Canadian Fun and Frolics

MAY

Banff Downhill Dummy Race - strap a dummy to some skis and hope it beats all the other contestants in this race. Say Natalie! Why don't we just strap Frank to some skis and enter him? No one would notice the difference!

N.G. 🔴🟤🔴🟤🔴

Follow that dummy!

JULY/AUGUST

The Buffalo Days Festival - A festival where people dress up in old-fashioned clothes and celebrate the old days. The best bit is definitely the Beard Growing Contest.

N.G. 🟤🔴🔴🟤🔴

89

AUGUST

Elk Island National Park's Great Buffalo-Chip Flip – This is my favourite. It's a frisbee-throwing contest with a difference. The contestants throw hardened cow flops and they make great frisbees because they're so flat and round! You win a prize for the longest throws.

F.P. ⓞⓞⓞⓞⓞⓞⓞⓞⓞⓞ

SEPTEMBER

The Great Klondike International Outhouse Race – they race old-fashioned toilets on wheels through Dawson City for three kilometres. One person sits on the john while four more push the outhouse – it's a big laugh! F.P. ⓞⓞⓞⓞⓞⓞⓞⓞ

ANYTIME

Cow Pie Bingo! – Our very own local wackytivity!
You can do it anytime, as long as there's no
snow on the ground! First we mark a field up
into numbered squares. Everyone chooses a
number. Now it gets real exciting! We let a cow
into the field and it starts munching the grass.
But – sooner or later it's going to have to drop
a flop of poo (yes, it's those country pancakes
again!) on to one of those squares. If it's your
square, you're the winner! But you'll probably
have to give your winnings to charity.

91

6 May

Hi! How're y' barkin'?

I'm having a pretty good time right now because Nat and me are in the Rockies with Mom and Bob in their RV. I guess I better tell you what an RV is, just in case you don't know. It's a motorized holiday home. They're real popular here and just perfect for touring our wildernormous places. RV is short for Recreational Vehicle, but I suppose it could also stand for Really Vast. Mom's is MASSIVE!

It's got a built-in kitchen, a shower, two bedrooms and a TV lounge. About the only

thing it hasn't got is its own front garden! But
when you've got scenery as stunning as the
Rocky Mountains all around, who needs one of
them! When we park up for the evening after
a day's rubbernecking (sightseeing) it feels like
we're still home! Mom says we're just four
wandering snails with one large luxury shell.

Today we've been to the Columbia Icefield.
Believe it or not, this mega-massive wodge of
ice is actually a left-over from the last Ice
Age. That was more than 20,000 years ago,
when the whole of Canada was covered by a
ginormous sheet of the stuff! The Columbia
Icefield still covers 325 square kilometres
and altogether it's got thirty different
glaciers!

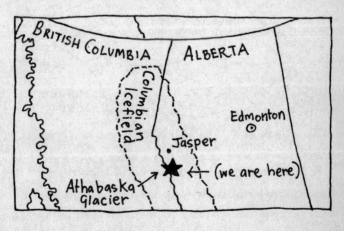

This morning we went to see the one called the Athabaska Glacier. Have you done glaciers at school yet? If you have, you'll know they're monster ice-sheets that form from snow at the top of mountains, and slide downhill because they're sooo heavy. As they go, they cut out eeenormous valleys in the side of the mountains. All this takes place r-e-a-l s-l-o-w.

New snow converts to glacial ice

How long's this ice taken to slither down the mountain?

Hmm... about six months?

Years out! This water fell as snow on the mountain top 175 years ago!

crevasses in the ice

Meltwater stream

So, glaciers don't exactly race along! And they aren't places to wander around on your own, either.

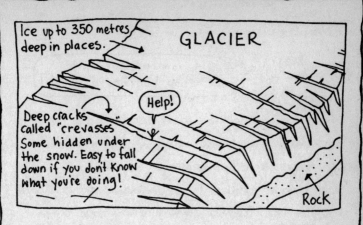

Instead of walking up the glacier and risking disappearing for all time we caught an 'ice big bus! (Ha!)

Awesome-and-three-quarters, eh? I'll write you again soon.

All the best,

Keri

7 May

Yodel ho and yodel ay ay to you ... hoo hoo hoo hooo ho!

That was my mountain echo in case you didn't knooowww! It's day two of our big chill-out in the even bigger Rockies! This morning we drove along the Ice Field Parkway, the highway that runs through the mountains. It's a real super-star of a road, about 230 kilometres long with non-stop, wow-making scenery all the way. I wish you could see it! People say it's the most beautiful drive on earth and they come from all over the world to do it. It's where Nature shows off its biggest and most megtacular creations!

We were all busy "Oohing" and "Aahing" at the towering peaks, sparkling lakes, flower-filled meadows and crashing waterfalls when Mom suddenly slammed on the RV's brakes! We soon saw why. Ambling across the road just a few metres in front of us was a black bear with her two furball cubs. Time for more "Oohs!" and "Aahs!".

Mom knows you have to drive extra careful in the Rockies because of all the wildlife that's about. She says that the wild animals have been following exactly the same trails for thousands and thousands of years. Just because some pesky humans decide to build a road across their pathway doesn't mean the animals'll change their habits. Hundreds of wild creatures are run over every year.

In the afternoon we went for a hike through Jasper National Park. Before we started we got prepared in case we ran into more bears. And I'm not talking teddies having picnics. We made sure we had these. . .

In case we ran into these. . .

black bears

Or maybe even these. . .

grizzlies

If you do accidentally bump into one they can turn real mean. No fun!

Aaaah!

And when they do there's no point in running away. These huge guys can run faster than the fastest Olympic runner . . . or even a racehorse!

So what you do is this.

We're heading home at the moment and after that 25 kilometre hike Nat and I are wiped out. As soon as I put my pen down I'm going to crash out on my bed and watch TV. And then - after Mom and Bob have dropped me back at Bison's Leap – I'll probably do the same again! But first, me and Nat are ready to hit you with part two of the Great Canadian Creature Feature, all about animals who live in the Rockies.

The Great Canadian Creature Feature
Part 2

GRIZZLY BEAR

– Their dark fur has yellowish tips so it looks grey. That's why they're called grizzly (another word for grey).

<u>Where found</u> – These big scary bears used to roam around the prairies killing and eating deer and bison but then the big wild herds got wiped out by the settlers, so they just stay in the mountains.

<u>Interesting facts</u> – When they stand on their back legs they can reach as high as four

metres! So if you climb a tree to escape from one make sure you climb up at least five metres!

They sleep for most of the winter and in the spring and summer they eat salmon and berries. The best wildlife thing we've ever seen was a family of them fishing for salmon at a waterfall. Luckily they were having too much fun to notice us.

WOLVES - These are really cool!

<u>Where found</u> - There used to be wolves all over Canada but lots of them were hunted and killed by settlers.

There are still quite a few about but now they mainly live in the forests as far away from humans as they can get.

<u>Interesting Facts</u> – A few years ago, when we were hiking through the woods in winter, we spotted three or four slinking through the trees just ahead of us. They looked just like ghosts, they were all shadowy. Spooky!

BIGHORN SHEEP – Named after its massive horns. The rams' horns grow extra-enormous and sometimes curl into a complete circle.

<u>Where found</u> – We see these all over the Rockies.

<u>Interesting facts</u> – If you count the rings on their horns you can work out how old they are – it's just like counting the age rings on tree trunks! When the male rams are sorting out who's going to be in charge of the flock they have head-banging battles. Owch!

COUGARS – The other name for these big cats is mountain lions or pumas.

<u>Where found</u> – They live in the Rockies and kill

deer for their food.

<u>Interesting facts</u> - They've been known to attack pet dogs and people but only when they're desperately hungry. There aren't too many about and most of the time they keep well away from humans which is sort of nice to know when you're out hiking in the woods.

CARIBOU -

They're a kind of reindeer.

<u>Where found</u> - We get a few of the woodland sort in the Rockies but in the cold arctic north there are masses more.

<u>Interesting facts</u> - In the fall the arctic ones gather in herds of up to 400,000 to migrate west to the forests for the winter. Dad says this is an awesome sight!

I'm real sad to say goodbye to Mum, but I guess I'll see her again soon.

Keri

29 May

Happy days to you, pen-pal!

Awesome news! Cindy's had her foal at last. It
was just after I got back from the Rockies.
We knew she was due any time and Dad and
Brad had been taking turns to sit up with her
at nights. Anyway, one lovely sunny afternoon, I
was just walking past her loose box when I
thought I'd take a peek in. And there she was!
Giving birth to her new foal!

He's three weeks old now and he's gorgeous.
And we've called him Snowberry, 'cos he's white
all over (like his dad). Him and Cindy are both
tearing around the meadow like mad things
below my bedroom window right now. The foal is
doing great leaps into the air and kicking his
heels like he'll take off and fly any moment!

I can't ride Cindy while she's looking after Snowberry, so Carol's loaned me her horse. He's an Appaloosa called Cherokee. He's quite a bit bigger than Cindy and he's a great runner. I went for a gallop across the prairie on him this afternoon. It was great, just like being in an old cowboy movie with the sheriff hot on my heels.

Do you ever watch old western movies? All that rootin' tootin' wild west action didn't only happen in the USA you know! It was real wild and lawless here in Alberta about a 130 years ago. You could do whatever you liked and you didn't have to worry about the cops. There weren't any! That's why the wicked whiskey traders came here from Montana after they'd been chased off by the American army. I've been checking them out for my history project. Seems they were very, very bad guys indeed!

Guess what they did when they got here? They built a trading fort so they could sell whiskey to the Indians and anyone else who wanted it. It wasn't the sort of whiskey Dad likes. They mixed up whiskey and water with stuff like ginger, red ink, chilli peppers . . . and they even added gunpowder to it! No wonder it was called firewater! The Indians paid for it with bison skins and horses.

The traders knew the explosive effect it had so they didn't let them in the fort. They made them push the skins through a slot in the wall (though I'm not too sure how they managed to hand over the horses?!). Then they passed them a bottle of whiskey back through the slot. Hmmph!

People started calling the trading post Fort

Whoop Up. Guess why! Yes, after the Indians and the other firewater fans had drunk their payment they whooped it up.

In the end the government thought things were getting a bit too wild so they sent a squad of cops to sort it out. They rode lovely chestnut coloured horses and dressed in red uniforms

(left over from the days of the British army) and were called the North West Mounted Police. They've been called the Mounties ever since! These heroes

marched hundreds of miles to Saskatchewan
and caught the guys who'd killed a group of
Indians. They then went on to get the whiskey
traders at Fort Whoop Up but the baddies were
long gone. So the Mounties brought law and
order to the wild west of Canada. People still say
today, "The Mounties always get their man!"

Alberta's generally pretty quiet nowadays.
Fort Whoop Up's been rebuilt as a tourist
centre and the modern Mounties drive around
in cars and don't even wear red uniforms

much. So if you do fancy a trip over here you can feel quite safe. The wildest thing you'll come across will probably be our marathon snowball battles.

Best wishes,

Keri

PS An Appaloosa is a spotty breed of horse. They were really popular with the Native Indians. Look out for them if you watch any old Western movies.

20 June

Hi pal!

Are you getting your summer heatwave yet? It was 27°C here today. And in a few weeks' time it'll be even hotter. Our crops are looking great and the prairies look like a really green sea, they're all covered with wheat! I can't believe it's just a few months since they were covered with 20 centimetres of snow!

OK! Here's today's news. Head Smashed In Buffalo Jump! No, I'm not being rude – that's the place that me and Natalie and her folks have been to visit today. Do you think it would like win a prize for one of the weirdest place-names on earth? I think it might! Unless you know some even weirder ones? Anyway, here's the amazing story of Head Smashed In Buffalo Jump.

Do you like my herd of bison? Bison is the proper name for the American buffalo. Once upon a time there were more than 60 million of these cuddlesome creatures roaming the prairies. And to the Native Indians, every one was like a walking superstore. They gave them meat for eating, skin for clothes, shoes, tents and bedclothes, dung for fuel, and bones and horns for tools, weapons and ornaments. Nothing was wasted.

Yup, thats just about everything!

Head Smashed In Buffalo Jump was surrounded by grassy plains – perfect bison-hunting country. Because thousands of them grazed there AND they lived about five miles from a really high cliff! Every year five hundred Blackfoot Indians had a huge hunt to stock up on food and stuff for the winter. These are some of the things they did to fool the bison:

1. They made lanes with walls built out of stones and branches, called drive lines, that would lead the bison to the edge of the cliff.

2. Some Indian runners dressed in wolf or bison skins and made calls to fool the bison so they'd walk into the lane.

3. The bison couldn't see too well, so they happily followed the furry Indians along the drive lines. The fools!

4. More Indians flapped bison skin blankets to keep the bison moving down the drive lines.

5. The bison would completely freak out and start to stampede along until they all ran over the cliff into a huge heap of dead and dying critters.

I've drawn it all for you below. Gross, eh? And it gets grosser. There are old buffalo jumps all over North America, but Head Smashed In is the most famous. Here's how it got its name. Once, a not very clever Blackfoot Indian hunter decided to stand at the bottom of the cliff to get a really great view of the buffalo coming over the top. You can guess what happened to him! After the Indians had cleared all the buffalo away, they found him right at the bottom of the pile – with his head all smashed in. Sorry about that.

Even though the history's gross, this place is sure worth a visit. It's at least 100 years since

113

the last stampede, but there's still a gi-
normous heap of bison bones and old Indian
weapons and stuff at the bottom of the cliff.
In the visitor centre you can see a video of
what the stampede must have
looked like. And in the cafe you
can get yourself a burger.
Yum!   What kind? Bison, of course! Enjoy!
    Guess what? There's a massive hail storm
going on outside right now,
with hailstones as big as
marbles. Sometimes
Alberta weather is
completely crazy!
Last-minute news
flash!! Snowberry's grown
15 centimetres in three
weeks. He's really shooting up!
    And finally, your next letter will be from a
surprise "guest writer" – see if you can guess
who!

Best wishes,

Keri

28 June

Hi,

I'm Frank Potter, Keri's friend. How you doing?
Are you into dinosaurs? I'm completely nuts
about them! And that's why Keri's asked me to
write you this letter.

When I grow up I'm going to be a
palaeontologist and spend all my time digging up
fossils and bones. And I'm really lucky to live in
Alberta, because it has to be the best place in the
world to be if you're as crazy about prehistoric
reptiles as I am. The whole of Red Deer River
Valley in south Alberta is full of dinosaur skeletons
and fossils and other cool bits and pieces.

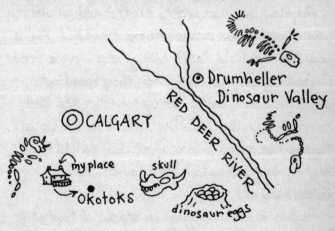

115

What's really surprising is that not long ago no one had a clue what all these bones and fossils

were! The Native Indians had like seen all the monster bones lying around for ages but they just decided they'd belonged to some sort of giant bison and thought no more about them.

Then, in 1884, a scientist took some of the huge bones back to his laboratory for a closer look and said,

WOW! These are real d-d-d-dinosaur bones ... YiPPEE!

Or something like that.

Anyway, he was pretty excited and so were a whole load of his palaeontologist buddies. You've heard of the Gold Rush? Well, there was a Great Canadian Dinosaur Rush when they found out what the bones were. Pretty soon the Red Deer River Valley was crawling with fossil freaks all digging like crazy. Guess what they called the first complete dinosaur they found? The Albertosaurus!

People are still digging up stacks of fantastic

prehistoric finds round here today. Every one they come up with seems to be more amazing than the last! Just before I was born a woman "rock hound" was poking around near her family's ranch when she found some dinosaur eggs that were 75 million years old. When the scientists checked them out they found perfectly formed baby dinosaur skeletons inside them. WOW! I wish it was me who found them.

Then, in 1995 a giant prehistoric whale was dug up in North Alberta. It was 100 million years old! I'm telling you! Jurassic Park's got nothing on us.

The Red Deer River valley is in the Alberta Badlands which looks like the kind of place where cowboy shoot-outs happen. Nothing much grows there and there's hardly any wildlife, just a few bob-cats and rattlesnakes (you've got to watch out for them when you're poking about for fossils!).

Bob-cat

Rattler

The reason all these great dinosaur finds have showed up is because millions of years ago stonking great glaciers moved down the valley carving away the rocks. After that the wind and rain and more ice and snow wore them down even more. It's still happening now. Every time it rains even more dinosaur bones turn up! More than 300 hundred complete dinosaur skeletons have been found so far. And yours truly is planning on finding a whole lot more! It's a great place to visit, whether you're a fossil freak or not.

OK – That's it. Let's saddle up and head 'em off at the pass then, Mack.

So long!

Your guest pen-palaeontologist,

Frank (South Alberta, Canada, The World)

15 July

Howdy Pen-Pardner,

YAHOO! It's me, Keri. And it's . . . RODEO TIME!
Tomorrow we're all going to Calgary, Alberta's
second biggest city, for the great Stampede.
Yes! It's the week when all the folks round here
go back 100 years in time and turn into old-
fashioned cowgirls and cowboys again. Then we
all have a whole lotta fun eating cowboy grits,
listening to country and western music and
watching top cowpokes show off their ropin' an'
ridin' skills! But of course, before all that, we
have to get ourselves gussied up to look the
part! So . . . we're putting on our cowboy boots
and a whole load of our dandiest rodeo gear.

People say the Calgary Stampede is the Greatest Show on Earth. I agree! The best action of all happens in the rodeo events at Stampede Park. Our ranch foreman, Wayne,

Howdy!

has entered them this year. He wants to win the $50,000 prize for the best cowboy. Dad says Wayne will either win the big money and give up working for us or get so badly hurt that he won't be able to work for us! Always looks on the bright side, my dad! Anyway, I'm going to be hollerin' for Wayne as he rides bucking broncos and ropes calves – and hopefully doesn't bite the dust! Way to go Wayne! But that's not all! Wayne's not the only one who entered in the rodeo. I have too! And Frank Potter. And my dare-devil brother, Brad. More on all this later.

I've made you this guide to some of the best events. I hope it gives you some idea of how awesome the Rodeo is. Maybe some day soon you'll come and see it for real!

RIDE 'EM COWBOYS...
AND COWGIRLS!

Wild cow milking – Brad (my brother) and Dave (Natalie's big brother) have gone in for this fun event this year. There's a herd of wild cattle in the middle of the ring. 20 teams with two men in each team race across to them and grab a cow. One man holds the cow while the other milks. The first team to get a couple of squirts of milk in their bucket and run across to the judges' table with it wins. This event's always a big laugh for the crowd. They hoot and holler all through for their favourite team!

Bareback bronco riding - Wayne's entered in this one. A bronco is a half-wild horse. Wayne will have to ride one without a saddle. As they both shoot out of the chute (!) he must keep his spurs above the horse's shoulders until its front hooves hit the ground - then he must stay on it for as long as he can (probably for about three seconds if he's lucky!)

Wayne ... (he did fall off a few seconds later)

Yeeha!

ride 'em cowboy!

The wild horse race - Another fun event for Brad and Dave with some help from Wayne. There are a herd of wild horses in the middle of the ring. They have to catch one, then get a saddle on it so that one of them can ride it and be first to the finishing line. But it hardly ever goes that smoothly!

Bull riding – This is the BIG one! It's full of thrills and spills and it's always held last. Wayne should do well at it – if he's still in one piece after his other events! All he has to do is to stay on the bull for just eight seconds. Doesn't sound long does it? Wayne told me it feels more like eight hours!

The bulls are meganormous and go completely crazy trying to shake the cowboy off their back. One of Wayne's hands will be sort of tied to the bull but he must keep the other one in the air all the time. Would I do that? No way!

OK! Have you decided which event you're going to enter when you come over here for the rodeo? Or do you just think you'll go for the whole lot? I'll write in a few days and let you know how Wayne and Brad got on . . . or off! Shucks! It's almost time to mosey on down to the old rodeo!

Uh oh! I almost forgot to tell you about my rodeo event. I'm going in for the Mutton Busting. It's a special competition for us kids. It's the one Frank's gone in for too. We have to ride a sheep across the ring. And stay on it . . . of course! Yes, it's going to be a really really wild and woolly ride! Sheep can be very awkward critters when they want to!

Yahoo!

Keri

24 July

Howdy pardner!

It's your Canadian sidekick, writing my very last
letter to you. How you moseying along? I suppose
you'll be wanting to know how I did in the rodeo.
Well, here are the results:

Brad Travis and Dave Green

Did quite well with the wild cow
milking – until the cow
kicked over the bucket
and began galloping
around with it hooked
on its horn. They gave
chase. Wild horse race a
dead loss. Brad stayed on for
at least 3 seconds . . . or was it 0.3 seconds?

Keri Travis

Didn't stay on my sheep for long. The belt
holding me on slipped and so did I. Bounce . . .
bounce . . . bounce! Right across the arena
(on my butt!). Got a real big laugh from the
crowd. Sheep – 6, K. Travis – 0

Frank Potter

Frank had better luck. He sort of managed to stay on his sheep but ended up leaning to one side and then the other side like this:

then sort of dangling like this:

and then (don't ask me how!) actually facing the wrong way like this:

The crowd loved him! The judges gave him a special "originality" prize. Ride 'em Frank!

Wayne Jameson

He did great in all of his events . . . until the wild bull riding! He got the biggest, meanest, orneriest bull in all Canada. The size of a snowplough!

He managed to stay on for . . . ooh . . . at least four seconds. When it threw him his hand stayed stuck in the cinch loop. The bull raced around the ring bellowing, tossing its head, snorting and pawing the ground, kicking its back legs in the air and all the time it was dragging poor old Wayne with it. I could hardly look! Then, just when I thought the monster was going to trample him to mush, the rodeo clowns rushed in and rescued him.

The rodeo clowns are great – they make things safe and provide everyone with a load of laughs too. Boy, was I glad to see 'em this time.

I'll stop writing now. I'm perched on three big cushions but sitting is still quite painful. I think I'll go for a walk around then maybe call Mom.

So, this is it! Time to say my last goodbye, for now. It's been great writing to you, pal. Miss Andrews thinks this project's been 100% successful and says she hopes that you've enjoyed reading my letters as much as she has! Now she says she wants me to think of an equally cool idea for next year. These teachers are never satisfied are they?

Natalie, Frank, Brad, Jodie and everyone all send their love.

Bye Bye!

Your pen-friend,

Keri

PS By the way, Cindy and Snowberry are doin' just fine. I'll be riding Snowberry this time next year!